Lucy's Loosey Toothy

For my Bug and Chasey Chase

Written by Heather Taylor Bradley
Illustrated by Tamara Marshall

There was a shark named Lucy who lived in the deep blue sea. She lived in a sunken ship with her family.

Lucy always woke up with a smile and brushed her teeth that were big and bright, but this morning Lucy had a loosey toothy that seemed to bother her day and night.

So Lucy went out swimming as she sang her little song,

"Loosey toothy, loosey toothy,
wiggle left and right,
loosey toothy, loosey toothy,
still too tight!"

Before long she came across Oscar Octopus, saying, "Let me help!"

With a wiggle, wiggle, wiggle, and a hug, hug, hug, Oscar Octopus tried to hug it out, but that tooth was still too snug.

So, Lucy went out swimming as she sang her
little song,

   "Loosey toothy, loosey toothy,
    wiggle left and right,
    loosey toothy, loosey toothy,
    still too tight!"

   Before long she came across Shelly Seahorse,
saying, "Let me help!"

   With a wiggle, wiggle, wiggle, and a tug, tug, tug,
Shelly Seahorse yanked that loosey toothy, but it just
wouldn't budge!

So Lucy went out swimming as she sang her little song,

   "Loosey toothy, loosey toothy,
   wiggle left and right,
   loosey toothy, loosey toothy,
   still too tight!"

Before long she came across Christy Crab, saying,
"Let me help!"

With a wiggle, wiggle, wiggle, and a pinch, pinch,
pinch, Christy Crab soon realized it wouldn't be a
cinch.

So Lucy went out swimming as she sang her little song,

"Loosey toothy, loosey toothy,
wiggle left and right,
loosey toothy, loosey toothy,
still too tight!"

9

Before long she came across Harry Hammerhead saying, "Let me help!"

With a wiggle, wiggle, wiggle, and a pound, pound, pound, Harry Hammerhead couldn't loosen it even jumping off the ground.

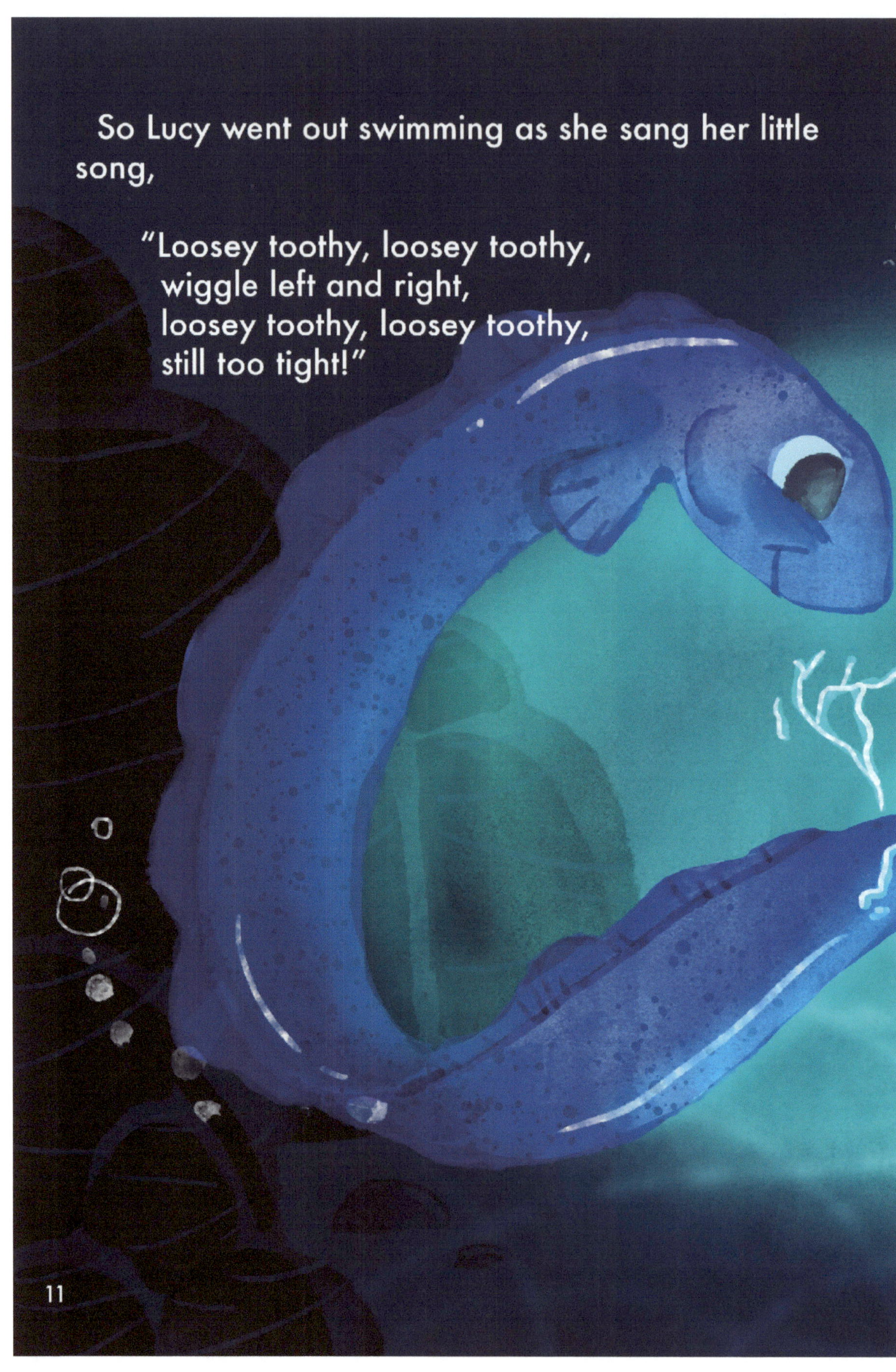

So Lucy went out swimming as she sang her little song,

"Loosey toothy, loosey toothy,
wiggle left and right,
loosey toothy, loosey toothy,
still too tight!"

Before long she came across Eli Electric Eel, saying,
"Let me help!"

With a wiggle, wiggle, wiggle, and a ZZZZ, ZZZZ,
ZZZZ, Eli Electric Eel tried to shock it out, but all that
did was leave Lucy's Bow in a frizz.

So her friends all gathered around her to think of another plan. "I know, I've got it! Just follow me!" said Chester, the old, trusted Clam. So, they followed Chester Clam into the Rainbow Reef Cafe.

"Why are we eating dinner when Lucy's toothy still isn't okay?"

"You'll see."

So with a wiggle, wiggle, wiggle, and a shake, shake, shake, Chester Clam sat back and smiled.

"Pepper is all it should take."

"AHHH, AHHH, AHHH,
CHOOEY!"

And with that big sneeze out flew Lucy's loosey toothy! It flew up to the ceiling as everyone gave a yell, and landed very safely in a nearby oyster shell.

So, Lucy took the shell home that held her tooth so tight and put it under her pillow for the shark fairy that night.

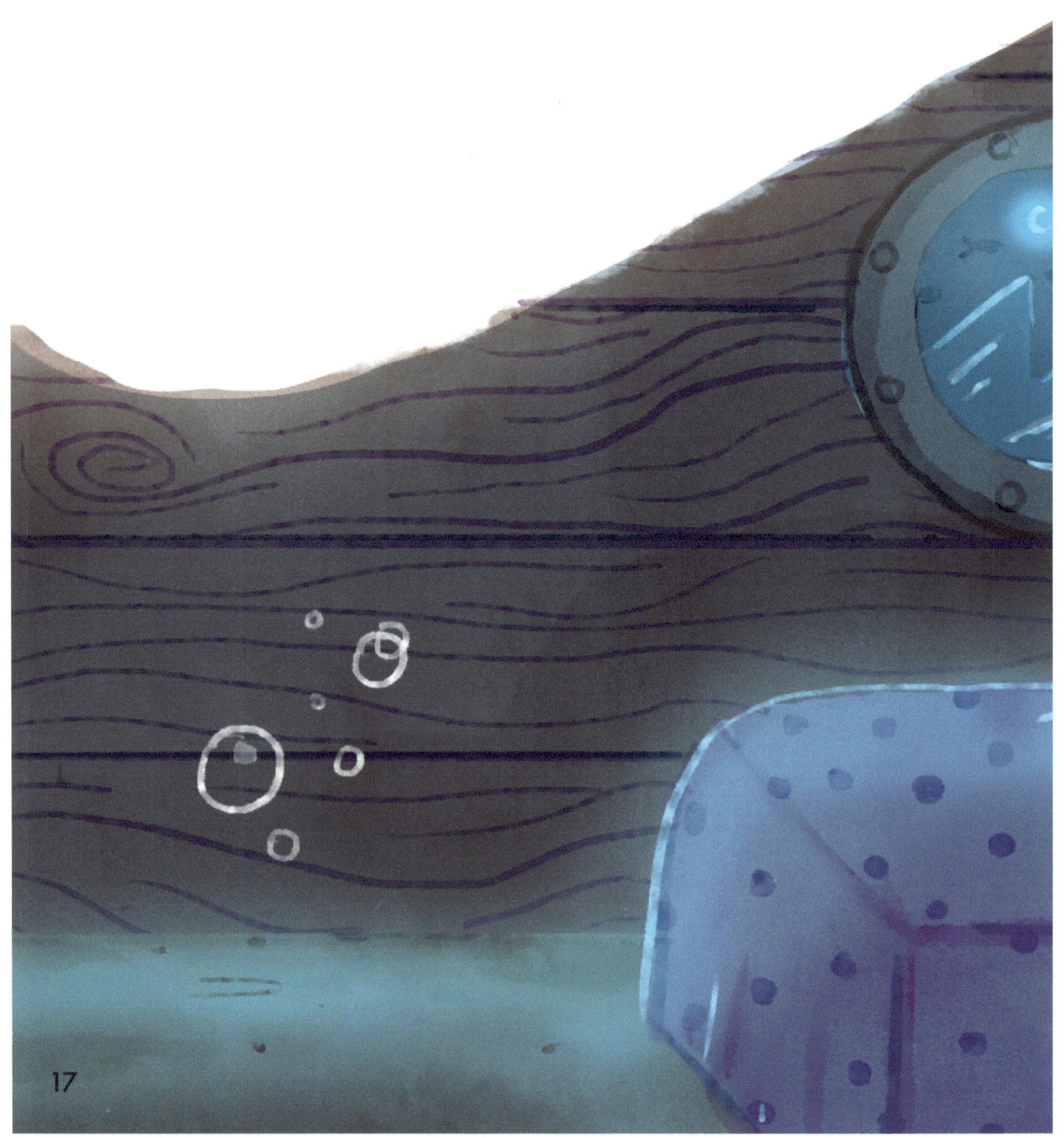

17

The moral of the story is simple and it is true. If you have a loosey toothy just let out a big...

AHHH, AHHH,

AHHH CHOO!

About the Author

Heather Taylor Bradley is a mother of two who lives in Ohio.

This is Heather's first published children's book. It has been her lifetime dream to have her books published and today that dream has come true.

When she is not writing, you can find her teaching Kindergarten, hiking with her dog, Jace (her favorite child), floating in her pool, texting her friend Emma, or finding any excuse to spend time with her two adult children.

Her family motto has always been to DREAM BIG! She would like to thank her two children, Gracyn and Chasen, for being her inspiration and to God for sustaining them every day. To God be ALL the glory. She would like to thank Him for the gift or writing. It has not always been easy but together they have made their dreams come true.

She would like to thank her VERY talented illustrator, Tamara Marshall, for taking a chance on her stories, seeing her vision and putting that vision to reality. Tamara has brought her characters to life in such a memorable way. She can't thank her enough.

Last, but certainly not least, she would like to thank her best friend Emma, for believing in her and giving her the confidence and kick in the butt to take that leap and make her dreams a reality. Her support and encouragement has made a lasting impression on her and she is so very thankful to call her a friend. Saggitearius and Gemini forever! She is thankful for going through this book publishing experience with her. Althought it has been a wild ride, she wouldn't want to go throught it with anyone else. You can hear Heather yell, "WE DID IT FRIEND, WE DID IT!"

About the Illustrator

Tamara Marshall has a background in illustration and recently graduated in Motion Desgin from Ringling College of Art and Design located in Sarasota, Florida.

She never dreamt that she would have the chance to work on a children's book and she's extremely grateful to Heather for the opportunity and for trusting her with her vision.

In her freetime Tamara enjoys curling up with a good book, (and a cat) swimming, hanging with friends, and jumping in puddles in the midst of a storm.

"God is good all the time, and all the time God is good." This has sustained and motivated her through all life's up and down's and reminded her to praise God in the storms. She would like to thank God for the ability to create and find the beauty in everything, even the mundane.

She would like to give a shout out to the people who taught and inspired her to learn art in the first place. Thank you to Cheryl Marshall, Cynthia Golden, and Ray Tomczak. Lastly she'd like to give a big hug to Gracyn Graley, whom she thanks for her friendship and without her none of this would be possible.